O9-AIE-494

2
WORDS
THAT WILL
CHANGE
YOUR LIFE
TODAY

Also by Joel Osteen

ALL THINGS ARE WORKING FOR
    YOUR GOOD
*Daily Readings from All Things Are
    Working for Your Good*

BLESSED IN THE DARKNESS
Blessed in the Darkness Journal
Blessed in the Darkness Study Guide

BREAK OUT!
Break Out! Journal
Daily Readings from Break Out!

EVERY DAY A FRIDAY
Every Day a Friday Journal
*Daily Readings from Every Day a
    Friday*

FRESH START
Fresh Start Study Guide

I DECLARE
*I Declare Personal Application
    Guide*

NEXT LEVEL THINKING
Next Level Thinking Study Guide
*Daily Readings from Next Level
    Thinking*

THE POWER OF I AM
The Power of I Am Journal
The Power of I Am Study Guide
*Daily Readings from The Power
    of I Am*

THINK BETTER, LIVE BETTER
Think Better, Live Better Journal
*Think Better, Live Better Study
    Guide*
*Daily Readings from Think Better,
    Live Better*

WITH VICTORIA OSTEEN
Our Best Life Together
Wake Up to Hope Devotional

YOU CAN, YOU WILL
You Can, You Will Journal
*Daily Readings from You Can,
    You Will*

YOUR BEST LIFE NOW
Your Best Life Begins Each Morning
Your Best Life Now for Moms
Your Best Life Now Journal
Your Best Life Now Study Guide
*Daily Readings from Your Best
    Life Now*
*Scriptures and Meditations for
    Your Best Life Now*
Starting Your Best Life Now

SOUTH PASADENA PUBLIC LIBRARY
1100 OXLEY STREET
SOUTH PASADENA, CA 91030

RELEASED FROM

2 WORDS
THAT WILL
CHANGE
YOUR LIFE
TODAY

JOEL OSTEEN

Faith
Words

New York • Nashville

Copyright © 2019 by Joel Osteen

Cover copyright © 2019 by Hachette Book Group, Inc.

Hachette Book Group supports the right to free expression and the value of copyright. The purpose of copyright is to encourage writers and artists to produce the creative works that enrich our culture.

The scanning, uploading, and electronic sharing of any part of this book without the permission of the publisher is unlawful piracy and theft of the author's intellectual property. If you would like to use material from the book (other than for review purposes), prior written permission must be obtained by contacting the publisher at permissions@hbgusa.com. Thank you for your support of the author's rights.

FaithWords
Hachette Book Group
1290 Avenue of the Americas
New York, NY 10104
faithwords.com
twitter.com/faithwords

First Edition: October 2019

FaithWords is a division of Hachette Book Group, Inc.
The FaithWords name and logo are trademarks of Hachette Book Group, Inc.

The publisher is not responsible for websites (or their content) that are not owned by the publisher.

The Hachette Speakers Bureau provides a wide range of authors for speaking events. To find out more, go to www.hachettespeakersbureau.com or call (866) 376-6591.

Literary development: Lance Wubbels Literary Services, Bloomington, Minnesota.

Print book interior design by Bart Dawson.

ISBN: 9781546038733 (hardback), 9781546038702 (ebook)

Printed in the United States of America
LSC-C
10 9 8 7 6 5 4 3 2 1

CONTENTS

Introduction 1

1. Two Powerful Words 5

2. Words Release God's Promises 27

3. Words Have Creative Power 57

4. Start Declaring Life-Changing Words . . 83

5. Speak Words of Blessing 97

INTRODUCTION

José Lima was a star pitcher for the Houston Astros during the late 1990s. One season he won twenty-one games and was considered one of the best pitchers in the league. But something interesting happened. When the Astros moved from the Astrodome to their new ballpark downtown, the fence in left field was much closer than the fence in the Astrodome, which, of course, favors the hitters. It makes it more difficult on the pitchers.

The first time Lima went to the new ballpark he walked onto the new diamond and stood on the pitcher's mound. When he looked out into left field and saw how close the fence was, the first words out of his mouth were, "I'll never be able to pitch in here. The fence is way too close."

Do you know he went from being a twenty-one-game winner to being a sixteen-game loser? It was one of the biggest negative turnarounds in Astros' history. What happened? The same thing that happens to many of us every day—we get what we say. Our words become self-fulfilling prophecies. If you allow your thoughts to defeat you and then give birth to negative ideas through your words, your actions will follow suit.

Words have incredible power. Whenever we speak something either good or bad, we give life to what we are saying. Unfortunately, too many people say negative things about themselves, about their families, and about their futures.

Here is the key: You have to send your words out in the direction you want your life to go. You cannot talk defeat and expect to have victory. You can't talk lack and expect to have abundance. You will produce what you say. If you want to know what you will be like five years from now, just listen to what you are saying about yourself. With our words we can either bless our futures or we can curse our futures.

I have written this book to tell you that there is a miracle in your mouth. If you want to change your life, start by changing your words. If you'll learn how to speak the right words and keep the right attitude, that allows God to do great things in your life.

You may be thinking, *This sounds too good to be true, Joel.* I know it's true! I've seen the power of our thoughts and words turn impossible situations into modern-day miracles.

Come on, let me tell you about it.

1

TWO POWERFUL WORDS

Lacy was a beautiful young lady who seemed to have everything going for her. She was smart, attractive, and came from a loving family. As we visited in the lobby after a service, she was friendly and had a pleasant personality. I thought if anybody would be happy, it would be her. But I soon realized it was just the opposite of what I thought. Lacy began to describe how she wasn't fulfilled, she was lonely, and she perceived her coworkers as more talented. She made statements such as, "I am unattractive. I am unlucky. I am a slow learner. I am always tired."

After five minutes of listening to Lacy, I knew exactly what was holding her back. Her "I am"s. What follows those two simple words will determine what kind of life you live. "I am blessed. I am strong. I am healthy." Or, "I am slow. I am unattractive. I am a lousy mother." The "I am"s coming out of your mouth will bring either success or failure.

All through the day the power of "I am" is at work. We make a mistake and out of our mouth tumbles, "I am so clumsy." We look in the mirror, shake our head, and say, "I am so old." We see somebody who we think is more talented and whisper under our breath, "I am so average." We get caught in traffic and grump, "I am so unlucky." Many times we wield the power of "I am" against ourselves. We don't realize how it's affecting our future.

Here's the principle. *Whatever follows the "I am" will eventually find you.* When you say, "I am so clumsy," clumsiness comes looking for you. "I am so old." Wrinkles come looking for you. "I am so overweight." Calories come looking for you. It's as though you're inviting them. Whatever you follow the "I am" with, you're handing it an invitation, opening the door, and giving it permission to be in your life.

The good news is you get to choose what follows the "I am." When you go through the day saying, "I am blessed," blessings come looking for you. "I am talented." Talent comes looking for you. You may not feel up to par, but when you say, "I am healthy," health starts heading your way. "I am strong." Strength starts tracking you down. You're inviting those things into your life.

That's why you have to be careful what follows the "I am." Don't ever say, "I am so unlucky. I never get any good breaks." You're inviting disappointments. "I am so broke. I am so in debt." You are inviting struggle. You're inviting lack.

You need to send out some new invitations. Get up in the morning and invite good things into your life. "I am blessed. I am strong. I am talented.

I am wise. I am disciplined. I am focused. I am prosperous." When you talk like that, talent gets summoned by Almighty God: "Go find that person." Health, strength, abundance, and discipline start heading your way.

But how many people, when they get up in the morning, look in the mirror and the first thing they say is, "I am so old. I am so wrinkled. I am so worn out." You are inviting oldness. You're inviting fatigue. Do us all a favor; stop inviting that. Dare to say, "I am young. I am energetic. I am vibrant. I am radiant. I am fresh. I am fearfully and wonderfully made." That's one of the best anti-aging treatments you could ever take, and it costs you nothing!

YOU ARE AN AMAZING, WONDERFUL MASTERPIECE

Some people have never once said, "I am beautiful. I am attractive." They're more focused on their flaws and what they don't like about themselves and how they wish they had more here and less there. When you say, "I am beautiful," beauty comes looking for you. Youth comes looking for you. Freshness comes looking for you. Nobody else can do this for you! It has to come out of your own mouth.

Ladies, don't go around telling your husband how unattractive you are. You should never put yourself down, and especially don't put yourself down in front of your husband. You are his prize. To him you are the most beautiful woman in the world. Why would you want to tell him anything different? The last thing he needs to hear is how bad you think you look. Don't put those negative thoughts in his mind. It's not going to do him or you any good to discredit yourself. If you keep telling him how bad you look, one day he may believe you.

But when you say, "I am beautiful," not only does beauty, youth, and freshness start coming your way, but on the inside your spirit person comes alive. Your self-image begins to improve, and you'll start carrying yourself like you're some-one special. You won't drag through the day feel-ing less than or inferior. You'll have that spring in your step, that "You go, girl!" attitude. Beauty is not in how thin or tall you are, how perfect you look. Beauty is in being who God made you to be with confidence. If you're a size 4, great. If you're a size 24, great. Take what you have and make the most of it.

God made you as you are on purpose. He gave you your looks, your height, your skin color, your nose, your personality. Nothing about you is by accident. You didn't get overlooked. You didn't get left out. God calls you His masterpiece. Instead of going around feeling down on yourself, too unattractive, too tall, too short, not enough of this, or too much of that, dare to get up in the morning and say, "I am a masterpiece. I am created in the image of Almighty God."

David said in Psalm 139, "God, I praise You because You have made me in an amazing way. What You have done is wonderful." Notice David's "I am"s. He was saying, not in pride but in praise to God, "I am wonderful. I am amazing. I am a masterpiece." That goes against human nature.

Most of us think, *There's nothing amazing about me. Nothing wonderful. I'm just average. I'm just ordinary.* But the fact is, there is nothing ordinary about you. You have a fingerprint that nobody else has. There will never be another you. Even if you have an identical twin, somebody who looks exactly like you, they don't have your same personality, your same goals, or even your same fingerprints. You are an original. When God made you, He threw away the mold. But as long as you go around thinking, *I'm just average. I'm just one of the seven billion people on the earth. There's nothing special about me,* the wrong "I am" will keep you from rising higher.

Rather than being down on ourselves and discrediting who we are and focusing on all of our flaws, I wonder what would happen if all through the day—not in front of other people but in private—we would be as bold as David was and say, "I am amazing. I am wonderful. I am valuable." When you talk like that, amazing comes chasing you down. Awesome starts heading in your direction. You won't have that weak, defeated "I'm just average" mentality. You'll carry yourself like a king, like a queen. Not in pride. Not being better than somebody, but with a quiet confidence, with the knowledge that you've been handpicked by the Creator of the universe and you have something amazing to offer this world.

GOD CAN EVEN
CHANGE YOUR NAME

That's what happened to a lady in the Scripture named Sarai. She had to change her "I am." God promised Sarai and her husband, Abram, that they would have a baby. But Sarai was eighty years old, way past the childbearing years. Back in those days, if a wife couldn't conceive and give her husband a child for some reason, even if it was the husband's fault, the wife was considered to be a failure. She was looked down on greatly. There was a sense of shame in not being able to conceive a baby. This is how Sarai felt. She was eighty years old and never had a baby. She felt as though she had let Abram down. Her self-esteem was so low. I can imagine some of her "I am"s: "I am a failure. I am inferior. I am not good enough. I am unattractive."

Yet Sarai has this promise from God that as an older woman she was going to have a baby. God knew that it would never come to pass unless He could convince Sarai to change her "I am"s. It was so imperative that she have this new mind-set that God actually changed her name from *Sarai* to *Sarah*, which means "princess."

Now every time someone said, "Good morning, Sarah," they were saying, "Good morning, Princess."

"How are you, Sarah?" "How are you, Princess?"

"Would you pass me the ketchup, Sarah?" "Would you pass me the ketchup, Princess?"

She heard this over and over. Those words got inside her and began to change her self-image. Sarah went from "I am a failure" to "I am a princess." From "I am unattractive" to "I am beautiful." From "I am ashamed" to "I am crowned by Almighty God." Instead of hanging her head in defeat, in embarrassment, she started holding her head up high. From "I'm not good enough" to "I am a child of the Most High God." From "I'm inferior" to "I am fearfully and wonderfully made." Her new attitude became: "I am amazing. I am wonderful. I am a masterpiece."

And ladies, as was true for Sarah, you may have had a lot of things in life try to push you down—bad breaks and disappointments, maybe people have tried to make you feel as though you just don't measure up or you're not quite attractive enough. You could easily let that seed get on the inside, ruin your sense of value, and cause you to live inferior. But God is saying to you what He said to Sarai, "I want you to change your name to Princess"—not literally, but in your attitude. You have to shake off the negative things people have said about you. Shake off the low self-esteem and the inferiority and start carrying yourself like a princess. Start walking like a princess. Start talking like a princess. Start thinking like a princess. Start waving like a princess!

Instead of whispering, "I am inferior. I am less than," you start declaring, "I am one of a kind. I am handpicked by Almighty God. I am valuable. I am a masterpiece." When you get up in the morning, don't focus on all your flaws. Look in the mirror and dare to say, "I am beautiful. I am young. I am vibrant. I am confident. I am secure." You may have had some disappointments. People may have tried to push you down, but quit telling yourself you're all washed up. Do as Sarah and say, "I am royalty. I am crowned with favor. I am excited about my future." This princess spirit got inside Sarah. It changed her self-image. I've learned you have to change on the inside before you'll see change on the outside. At ninety-one years old, against all odds, she gave birth to that baby. The promise came to pass.

SO WHAT'S COMING OUT OF YOUR MOUTH?

My question today is, What kind of "I am"s are coming out of your mouth? "I am victorious. I am blessed. I am talented. I am anointed." When you have the right "I am"s, you're inviting the goodness of God. Maybe if you would just change the "I am," you would rise to a new level. Words have creative power. They can be very helpful, like electricity. Used the right way, electricity powers lights, air-conditioning, and all kinds of good things.

But electricity used the wrong way can be very dangerous. It can harm you, even kill you. It's the same way with our words. Proverbs 18:21 says, "Life and death are in the power of our tongue." It's up to you to choose what follows the "I am." My encouragement is to never say negative things about yourself. Most of us would never go up to another person, at least to their face, and criticize them, yet we have no problem criticizing ourselves. "I am so slow. I am so unattractive. I am so undisciplined." That is cursing your future. Do yourself a favor and zip that up. We have enough in life against us already. Don't be against yourself.

I had a friend with whom I used to play basketball. When he would miss an important shot, he would exclaim, "I'm an idiot! I'm an idiot! I'm an idiot!" I heard that month after month. He didn't realize it, but "idiot" was coming, looking for him. I hate to say it, but I think it found him!

If you go around saying, "I am so dumb," this may be poor English, but "dumbness" is coming your way. "I am so unattractive. I am so plain." Ugliness says, "I hear somebody calling my name." Use your words to bless your future, not curse your future.

The Scripture says, "Let the weak say, 'I am strong'"—not the opposite, "I am so tired. I am so run-down." That's calling in the wrong things.

Let the poor say, "I am well off"—not, "I am broke. I am so in debt."

Let the sick say, "I am healthy. I am improving. I am getting better and better."

YOU ARE WHO
GOD SAYS YOU ARE

Romans 4 says to "call the things that are not as though they were." That simply means that you shouldn't talk about the way you are. Talk about the way you want to be. If you're struggling in your finances, don't go around saying, "Oh, man, business is so slow. The economy is so down. It's never going to work out." That's calling the things that are as if they will always be that way. That's just describing the situation. By faith you have to say, "I am blessed. I am successful. I am surrounded by God's favor."

I asked a young man recently how he was doing in high school. He said, "I'm doing okay. I'm just a C student." Come to find out, when he was back in elementary school, one of his teachers told him he was a C student, and he let that seed take root and bloom. I told him what I'm telling you. As long as you're saying, "I am a C student," you're not going to become an A student. You're calling in the C's, and those C's will come find you wherever you go. If you're not careful, you'll make a C in homeroom, a C in lunch, and C in PE. Change the "I am." "I am an A student. I am smart. I am full of wisdom. I am a good learner. I am excellent."

Have you allowed what somebody—a coach, a teacher, a parent, an ex-spouse—said about you to hold you back? They've planted negative seeds of what you cannot do. "You're not smart enough. You're not talented enough. You're not disciplined enough. You're not attractive enough. You'll always make C's. You'll always be mediocre. You'll always struggle with your weight." Get rid of those lies! That is not who you are. You are who God says you are.

People may have tried to push you down and tell you who or what you can't become. Let that go in one ear and out the other ear. What somebody said about you doesn't determine your destiny: *God does*. You need to know not only who you are but also who you are not. In other words, "I am not who people say I am. I am who God says I am. I am not the tail; I am the head. I am not a borrower; I am a lender. I am not cursed; I am blessed."

As was true in this young man's life, somebody may have spoken negative words to you when you were young. But know this: Before anyone could put a curse on you, God put a blessing on you. Before you were formed in your mother's womb, God knew you, and He approved you. When God made you, He stepped back and said, "I like that. That was good. Another masterpiece!" He stamped His approval on you. Other people may try to disapprove you. Don't go around feeling less than, feeling inferior. Our attitude should be: *I am approved by Almighty God. I am accepted. I am a masterpiece.* When you talk like that, the seeds of greatness God has placed inside will begin to spring forth.

CHANGE YOUR "I AM"S

You have gifts and talents that you've not tapped into yet. There is a treasure inside you. Throughout life, negative thoughts will try to keep it pushed down. The enemy doesn't want you to reach your full potential. There are forces constantly trying to make you feel intimidated, inferior, inadequate. If you're going to fulfill your destiny, you have to shake off the negative voices. Shake off the thoughts that are telling you, *I am unable. I am unqualified.* Don't invite weakness. Don't give intimidation an invitation. You may feel unqualified, but before you were born, God equipped you. He empowered you. You are not lacking anything. God has already stamped His approval on you. People may try to push you down, but when you know God has approved you, you realize, *I don't need other people's approval. I've been equipped, empowered, and anointed by the Creator of the universe!*

I know a man who was told by his high school counselor that he wasn't very smart and should focus on the lowest skilled job that he could find. I'm sure the counselor meant well, but he didn't know who this young man was on the inside. He didn't see the seeds of greatness God had planted in this young man. As a high school student, this young man's "I am" was distorted. "I am not up to par. I am not smart. I am very average." He didn't realize he was inviting that into his life, but over time it showed up.

After high school, this man got a job at the local factory and stayed at the lowest level year after year after year. One day the factory closed down, so he went across town and applied at another factory. This company had a policy that job applicants had to first take an IQ test. He took the test and scored the highest in the company's sixty-three-year history. His IQ score was assessed at genius level. He went on to start his own business, and he invented and patented two very successful products. Today, he is extremely blessed.

What happened? He changed his "I am."

Could it be what someone has told you is keeping you from God's best? Could it be that the wrong "I am" is keeping you from rising higher and reaching your full potential? Do what this man did. Change your "I am." Don't let what somebody told you determine your destiny. Get in agreement with God. Know who you are and know who you are not. "I am not lacking. I am not average. I am not inferior. I am equipped. I am empowered. I am anointed. I am wise. I am a masterpiece."

BE A JOSHUA, BE A CALEB

In Numbers 13, Moses sent twelve men in to spy out the Promised Land. After forty days, ten of them came back and said, "Moses, we don't have a chance. The cities are fortified and very large and the people are huge. Compared to them we felt like we were grasshoppers." Notice their "I am"s. "I am weak. I am inferior. I am intimidated. I am afraid." What happened? Fear, intimidation, and inferiority came knocking at their door.

The other two spies, Joshua and Caleb, came back with a different report. They said, "Moses, yes, the people are big, but we know our God is much bigger. We are well able. Let us go in and take the land at once." Their "I am"s were just the opposite. "I am strong. I am equipped. I am confident. I am more than a conqueror."

What is interesting is that the negative report from the ten spies spread like wildfire throughout the rest of the camp. Before long some two million people were intimidated and afraid. Nobody even paid attention to Joshua and Caleb's report of faith. Here's what I've learned: A negative report always spreads faster than a positive report. When people are murmuring, complaining, and talking defeat, be on guard. Make sure you don't let the wrong "I am" take root.

The people of Israel were so distressed by the negative report that they complained against Moses and Aaron, "Why did you even bring us out here? We're going to die in the wilderness. Our children, our wives, they're going to be taken as plunder."

God answered back something very powerful and very sobering. He said in Numbers 14, "I will do for you exactly what you have said. You said you're going to die in the wilderness, so you will die in the wilderness." God is saying the same thing to us. "I am going to do exactly what you've been saying." Don't ever say, "I am weak. I'm intimidated. I'm inferior." Friend, the wrong "I am" can keep you from your destiny.

Do you remember reading in the Scripture about a man named Sethur, a man named Gaddi, or a man named Shaphat? I'm fairly certain that you've never heard of them. You know why? They were listed among the ten spies who brought the negative report. They also never made it into the Promised Land. The fact is they were called to be history makers, just as Joshua and Caleb were. They had seeds of greatness inside them, but the wrong "I am" kept them from making their mark.

Don't let that be your destiny. You may be facing some major obstacles. My challenge is for you to be a Joshua. Be a Caleb. "I am strong. I am confident. I am equipped. I am more than a conqueror. I am well able." Make sure you have the right "I am"s coming out of your mouth.

Joshua and Caleb were the only two from that whole wilderness company to ever make it into the Promised Land.

SPEAK THESE "I AM"S OVER YOUR LIFE

Let me give you some "I am"s to speak over your life. Read over these declarations every day. Get them down in your spirit. Meditate on them. They may not all be true right now, but as you continue to speak them, they will become a reality.

"I am blessed. I am prosperous. I am successful."

"I am victorious. I am talented. I am creative."

"I am wise. I am healthy. I am in shape."

"I am energetic. I am happy. I am positive."

"I am passionate. I am strong. I am confident."

"I am secure. I am beautiful. I am attractive."

"I am valuable. I am free. I am redeemed."

"I am forgiven. I am anointed. I am accepted."

"I am approved. I am prepared. I am qualified."

"I am motivated. I am focused. I am
    disciplined."

"I am determined. I am patient. I am kind."

"I am generous. I am excellent. I am equipped."

"I am empowered. I am well able."

"I am a child of the Most High God."

2

WORDS RELEASE
GOD'S PROMISES

You are where you are today in part because of what you've been saying about yourself. Words are like seeds. When you speak something out, you give life to what you're saying. If you continue to say it, eventually that can become a reality. Whether you realize it or not, you are prophesying your future. This is great when we're saying things such as, "I'm blessed. I'm strong. I will accomplish my dreams. I'm coming out of debt." That's not just being positive; you are actually prophesying victory, prophesying success, prophesying new levels. Your life will move in the direction of your words.

But too many people go around prophesying just the opposite. "I never get any good breaks." "I'll never get back in shape." "Business is slow. I'll probably get laid off." "Flu season is here. I always get it." They don't realize they are prophesying defeat. It's just like they're calling in bad breaks, mediocrity, and lack.

The Scripture says, "We will eat the fruit of our words." When you talk, you are planting seeds. At some point, you're going to eat that fruit. My challenge is: Make sure you're planting the right kind of seeds. If you want apples, you have to sow apple seeds. If you want oranges, you can't plant cactus seeds, poison ivy seeds, or mushroom seeds. You're going to reap fruit from the exact seeds that you've been sowing. In other words, you can't talk negative and expect to live a positive life. You can't talk defeat and expect to have victory. You can't talk lack, not enough, can't afford it, never get ahead and expect to have abundance. If you have a poor mouth, you're going to have a poor life.

If you don't like what you're seeing, start sowing some different seeds. Instead of saying, "I'll never get well, Joel. This sickness has been in my family for three generations," plant the right seeds by stating, "God is restoring health back unto me. This sickness didn't come to stay; it came to pass. I'm getting better and better every day." You keep sowing those positive seeds and eventually you'll eat that abundant fruit—health, wholeness, victory.

Instead of saying, "I'll never get out of debt. I'll never rise any higher," you start speaking the promises of God: "I will lend and not borrow. Whatever I touch prospers and succeeds. I'm coming into overflow, into more than enough." Start sowing seeds of increase, seeds of abundance. No more "I'll never accomplish my dreams." Instead, "I have the favor of God. Blessings are chasing me down. The right people are searching me out. New opportunities, new levels are in my future." If you'll keep talking like that, you'll reap a harvest of good things.

START BLESSING YOUR LIFE

The Scripture talks about how with our tongue we can bless our life or we can curse our life. Many people don't realize they're cursing their future with their words. Every time you say, "I never get any good breaks," you just cursed your life. "I'll never be able to afford that nice house." "I'll never be able to break this addiction." "I'll never meet the right person." No; stop cursing your future. Sometimes the enemy doesn't have to defeat us; we defeat ourselves. Pay attention to what you're saying. Are you blessing your life? Or are you cursing it?

I had a classmate in high school who was always very negative even though he was one of the stars on our football team, was always in great shape, and had thick, curly hair. Every time I asked him what was going on, he gave this standard reply: "Not much. I'm just getting old, fat, and bald." I must have heard him say that five hundred times. I know he was just kind of kidding, but I wouldn't kid about that. About fifteen years later, when I ran into him at the mall, I nearly passed out. He had prophesied his future. He looked old, fat, and bald. Don't speak that defeat over your life. Our attitude should be, *I'm getting younger. God is renewing my youth like the eagles. I'm getting stronger, healthier, better looking. I'm going to keep my hair. I'm going to stay in my right mind. I'm going to live a long, productive, faith-filled life.* Don't go around cursing your future. Start blessing your life. Prophesy good things.

I know this man who was so concerned that he was going to get Alzheimer's disease because several people in his family had it—a grandfather, a great-uncle. This man was only in his early fifties, but he constantly kept bringing up what might happen. He told me that he was actually making plans for someone to take care of him, getting everything lined up. Of course, it's good to use common sense, to be wise, and to plan ahead in your life where you can. But if you go around talking about when you're going to get a disease and making plans for it, you probably won't be disappointed. You're calling it in. Just like you're sending it an invitation.

I told this man what I'm telling you: "Don't say another time that you're going to have Alzheimer's or any other disease. Start declaring, 'No weapon formed against me will ever prosper. I will live out my days in good health, with a clear mind, with good memory, with clarity of thought. My mind is alert. My senses are sharp. My youth is being renewed.'" You must prophesy health. Prophesy a long, productive life. Your words will become your reality.

DON'T GET TRAPPED BY OWN YOUR WORDS

Proverbs 6 states, "We are snared by the words of our mouth." *Snared* means "to be trapped." Your words can trip you. What you say can cause you to stumble and keep you from your potential. You're not snared by what you think. Negative thoughts come to us all. But when you speak them out, you give them life. That's when they become a reality. If you say, "I'll never get back in shape," it becomes more difficult to get back in shape. You just made it harder. When you say, "I never get any good breaks," you stop the favor that was ordained to you. If you say, "I'm not that talented. I don't have a good personality," you're calling in mediocrity. It's setting the limits for your life. When negative thoughts come, the key is to never verbalize them. That thought will die stillborn if you don't speak it.

When we acquired the former Compaq Center, it was a dream come true. We were so excited. Our architects drew up plans to change it from a basketball arena to a church. They called us together and said it was going to cost one hundred million dollars to renovate! After they picked me up off the floor, my first thoughts were, *That's impossible! There's no way! I've only been the pastor four years. They cannot expect me to raise those kinds of funds.* Even though those thoughts were racing through my mind again and again, I knew enough to keep my mouth closed. I kept a big smile on my face and acted as though it was no big deal. I knew if I wouldn't verbalize those negative thoughts, eventually they would die stillborn. It's one thing to think that it's impossible, but when you start telling people something's impossible, it takes on a whole new meaning.

You may think, *I'll never get that job. I'll never get well. I'll never meet the right person.* Those thoughts come to all of us. You can't stop that. My challenge is: Don't give them life by speaking them out. Don't go call your friends and tell them how it's not going to happen. I told our team, "I don't see a way, but I know God has a way. He didn't bring us this far to leave us." My report was: "God is supplying all of our needs. The funds are coming in. It may look impossible on paper, but with God all things are possible." I knew better than to curse my future. I didn't want to get trapped by my words. I knew if I kept prophesying the right things—increase, favor, more than enough—we would start moving toward it, and we did!

In the tough times, you have to especially be on guard. It's very tempting to vent your frustration and tell people how the loan didn't go through, how bad the medical report was, or how certain people just didn't treat you right. When you continually talk about the problem, that's only going to make you more discouraged, and it gives that problem more life. You're making it bigger. Turn it around. Don't talk about the problem; talk about the promise.

Instead of complaining, "Oh, man, I've got this big challenge," state, "I serve a big God. He spoke worlds into existence. Nothing's too difficult for Him."

Instead of surmising, "I didn't get the promotion they promised. They passed over me again. Another disappointment," declare, "I know when one door closes that means God has something better. He's directing my steps. I'm excited about my future."

Instead of concluding, "I'll never meet the right person. I'm too old. It's been too long," state, "Something good is going to happen to me. Divine connections are coming my way."

When someone says, "I'm sorry to hear that you got a bad medical report. Is it true?" you should respond, "Yes, that's true. But I have another report that tells me God is restoring health back unto me."

If your friend remarks, "Well, I heard those

people did you wrong," feel free to smile, nod your head, and explain, "Yes, but I'm not worried. God is my vindicator. He's fighting my battles. He's promised to give me beauty for ashes."

TWO VOICES—WHICH ONE ARE YOU CHOOSING?

In life, there are always two voices competing for your attention—the voice of faith and the voice of defeat. Just as I did, you'll hear a voice piping in, "You can't possibly raise that amount of money. It's insurmountable. It's not going to work out. Just accept it." You'll be tempted to worry, to be negative, to complain. But if you listen carefully, you'll hear another voice. The voice of faith is saying, "God has a way. Favor is coming. Healing is coming. Breakthroughs are coming."

One voice will point out that you've reached your limits. You've gone as far as you can. You don't have what it takes. The other voice is clear and matter-of-fact: "You are well able. You can do all things through Christ. Your best days are still out in front of you." Now, here's the beauty. You get to choose which voice comes to life. The way you do it is by what you speak. When you verbalize that thought, you're giving it the right to come to pass. If you mope around saying, "The problem's too big. I'll never get well," you are choosing the wrong voice. You have to get in agreement with God. The other voice may seem louder, but you can override it. You can take away all of its power by choosing the voice of faith.

Maybe you're going to a job interview. One voice will warn you, "You're not going to get it. You're wasting your time. These people are not going to like you." Another voice will counter, "You have the favor of God. You're blessed. You're confident. You have what it takes." If you get up that morning and tell your spouse, "I don't think I'm going to get this job. They're not going to like me. I'm not qualified," there's no use in you going. You're being trapped by your words. You have to dig your heels in and say, "I am not giving life to any more defeat. I am not speaking lack. I'm not speaking sickness. I'm not speaking mediocrity, fear, doubt. I can't do it.

I'm choosing the voice of faith. It says I am strong, I am healthy, and I am blessed. I am favored. I am a victor and not a victim."

God gave Jeremiah a promise that he would become a great prophet to the nations (Jeremiah 1). But when he heard God's voice, he was very young and unsure of himself. He instead listened to the other voice and said, "God, I can't do that. I can't speak to the nations. I'm too young. I wouldn't know what to say."

God said, "Jeremiah, say not that you are too young."

The first thing God did was to stop his negative words. Why did God do that? Because He knew that if Jeremiah went around saying, "I'm not qualified. I can't do this. I don't have what it takes," he would become exactly what he was saying. So God said in effect, "Jeremiah, zip it up. You may think it, but don't speak it out loud." It goes on to tell how Jeremiah changed what he was saying, and he became a prophet to the nations. The promise came to pass.

In the same way, God has called every one of us to do something great. He's put dreams, desires on the inside, but it's easy to acquiesce as Jeremiah did and say, "I can't do that. I'm too young. I'm too old. I've made too many mistakes. I don't have the education. I don't have the experience." We can all make excuses, but God is saying to us what He said to Jeremiah, "Stop saying that." Don't curse your future. Those negative words can keep you from God's best.

NEGATIVE WORDS STOP GOD'S PROMISES

Sometimes the reason a promise is being delayed is because of what we're saying. Imagine that your answer is on the way. God has already dispatched the angel with your healing, your promotion, your vindication. But right before it arrives, God says to the angel, "Hold on. Don't go any farther. Stay right where you are."

The angel replies, "Why, God? This is what You promised. It's in Your Word."

God answers, "No, listen to what he's saying. He's talking about how it's not going to happen, how the problem is too big, how it's been too long, how he'll never meet the right person."

Negative words stop God's promises. I wonder how many times we're just a couple of months away from seeing the answer, a couple of months from meeting the right person. You've been praying for years that God would bring somebody great into your life. But right before they show up, you let your guard down and start saying, "Oh, it's not going to happen. I'm too old. Nobody's interested in me." God has to say to the angel, "Don't go any farther."

The good news is that promise is still in your future. God didn't cancel it because you got negative. He still has the right person for you, and if you'll zip up the doubt and switch over into faith, at the right time, that person will show up. God will release what negative words have delayed. God still has your healing, your promotion, your restoration. Now do your part. Quit talking about how it's not going to happen. You may not see a way, but God still has a way. It may look impossible, but God can do the impossible. Just because you don't see anything happening doesn't mean God is not working. Right now, behind the scenes, God is arranging things in your favor. He is lining up the right people. He is moving the wrong people out of the way. He is positioning you exactly where He wants you to be. Now don't delay the promise by speaking negative words.

When our son, Jonathan, was seventeen years old, we were in the process of applying to different colleges. Some schools only accept 5 percent of the students who apply. That means, of course, that 95 percent of the applicants get turned down. It's easy to think, *Why do we even want to apply to those schools? It's practically impossible to get in. More than nine out of ten students get denied. Jonathan, don't get your hopes up. I don't see how you could get in there.*

If we're not careful, we'll talk ourselves out of it. You may think those thoughts, but don't make the mistake of verbalizing them. Learn to turn it around. "God, I know You have my son in the palm of Your hand. You've already picked out the right college for him to attend. There may be only a 5 percent chance for some schools, but God, I know that with You there's a 100 percent chance he will get in exactly where You want him to go. God, You control the whole universe."

That's much better than going around saying, "All the odds are against me. It doesn't look good. I don't see how it's going to happen." No, zip that up. If you can't be positive, at least be quiet. Your words prophesy your future. If you say, "I'll never get in," you're right; you'll never get in. If you say, "This problem is going to sink me," it will take you under. If you say, "I'll never be able to afford a nice house," you'll never be able to afford a nice house. You're being snared by the words of your mouth.

PUT A WATCH OVER YOUR MOUTH

In the first chapter of Luke, an angel appeared to a priest named Zechariah while he was serving in the temple. The angel told him that his wife, Elizabeth, was going to have a baby and they were to name him John. Zechariah was very surprised, because he and his wife were way up there in years. He said to the angel, "Are you sure this is going to happen? It sounds great, but do you see how old we are? To me, it just doesn't seem possible."

The angel said, "Zechariah, I am Gabriel. I stand in the presence of Almighty God, and what God says will come to pass."

God knows the power of our words. He knew that if Zechariah went around speaking defeat, it would stop His plan. So God did something unusual. The angel said, "Zechariah, because you doubted, you will remain silent and not be able to speak until the baby is born." Zechariah left the temple unable to talk; he couldn't speak one word for nine months, until that baby was born.

Why did God take away Zechariah's speech? God knew he would go out and start telling his friends how it wasn't going to happen. "Hey, man. This angel appeared and said we're going to have a baby. He must have the wrong person. We're too old." Those negative words would have stopped his destiny. That's why the Scripture says, "Put a watch over your mouth." In other words, "Be careful what you allow to come out of your mouth."

"I don't think I'm ever going to get well. I've had this sickness for three years." No; put a watch over your mouth. Don't prophesy that defeat. If you're going to say anything, declare what God says: "I will live and not die. God is restoring health back unto me. The number of my days He will fulfill." All through the day you need to ask yourself, "Is what I'm about to say what I want to come into my life?" Because what you're saying, you're inviting in.

When you say, "I'll never pay off my house and get out of debt. The economy is too slow," you're inviting struggle and lack. When you say, "My career has dead-ended. This is as good as it gets," you're inviting defeat and mediocrity. You need to send out some new invitations. When you say, "I will lend and not borrow. God's favor surrounds me like a shield. Whatever I touch prospers and succeeds," you are inviting increase, good breaks, and success. When you say, "I will overcome this problem. I am more than a conqueror. If God be for me, who dare be against me?" you're inviting strength, healing, restoration, vindication, and breakthroughs.

Pay attention to what you're inviting. "I'll never pass this algebra course. I've never been good in math. I just don't understand it." Change the invitation. "I can do all things through Christ. I have good understanding. I am full of wisdom. I am an A student." When you do that, you're inviting wisdom and an acceleration of knowledge. You're inviting God's blessings. Make sure you're sending out the right invitations.

When I first started ministering back in 1999, I had never done this before, and I was very nervous and unsure of myself. Negative thoughts bombarded my mind: *Joel, you're going to get up there and make a fool of yourself. You're not going to know what to say. Nobody is going to listen to you. Why should they? You don't have the experience.* All through the day I had to ignore those thoughts. I would go around saying under my breath, "I am anointed. I am equipped. I am strong in the Lord." Before I would come to church and minister, I would look at myself in the mirror and say, "Joel, you are well able. You've been raised up for such a time as this."

I didn't feel confident, but I called myself confident. I didn't feel anointed, but I called myself anointed. You may not feel blessed, but you need to call yourself blessed. The circumstances may not say you're prosperous, but by faith you need to call yourself prosperous. You may not feel healthy today, but don't go around telling everyone how you're not going to make it. Start calling yourself healthy, whole, strong, full of energy and full of life.

WHEN MARCHING AROUND WALLS, ZIP IT UP

When Joshua was leading the people of Israel toward the Promised Land, they came to the city of Jericho. It towered between them and their destiny. They couldn't go around it. They had to

go through it. The problem was: Jericho was surrounded by huge, thick, tall walls made up of stone
and mortar. It didn't look as though there was any
way the Israelites could get in. But God told them
to do something that sounded strange—for six days
they were to march around those walls once a day,
and on the seventh day they were to march around
them seven times. If that wasn't odd enough, God
gave them one final instruction, which was the
key to the whole plan working. He said, "While
you're marching around the walls, I don't want you
to say one word, not a whisper, not a short conversation, not an update on how it's going. Keep
totally silent."

Why did God not allow them to speak? God
knew that after a couple of times around the perim-
eter of the walls, if not before they even started
marching, they would be saying, "What in the
world are we doing out here? These walls are never
going to fall. Look how thick they are. They've been
here forever. Joshua must have heard God wrong."
Somebody else speaks up, "Yeah, and I'm tired. I'm

hot. I'm hungry. This dust is getting in my face."
God knew they would talk themselves out of it.
There are times in all of our lives where it's difficult to be positive. And that's okay. Just stay silent.
Don't tell everyone what you're thinking. The
people of Israel marched in silence, and you know
how the story ends. On the seventh time around
on the seventh day the walls came tumbling down.

Here's the question today: Could it be that negative words are keeping you out of your Promised
Land? Could it be that if you would remain silent,
that if you would zip it up and not talk about how
big the problem is, not complain about what didn't
work out, not tell a friend how you're never going
to be successful, maybe the walls that are holding
you back would come down? Imagine behind those
walls are your healing, your promotion, your dream
coming to pass. Every day, so to speak, you're walking around the walls. What are you saying? "This
wall is never going to fall, Joel. I've had this addiction since high school." "I'll never be able to start
my own business. I don't know the right people."

God is saying to us what He said to the Israelites: "If you can't say anything positive and full of faith, don't say anything at all." Don't let your negative words keep you from God's best. If you'll stop talking defeat, lack, how it's not going to happen, and simply remain silent, God can do for you what He did for them. He knows how to bring those walls down.

When we're marching around the walls, sometimes we go day after day and don't see anything happening. Just like the Israelites, the thoughts come swirling around our heads: *You didn't hear God right. Nothing is changing. You go to work every week and do your best, but you're not being promoted, and it's never going to happen.* No, that is a time of testing. Like the Israelites, you're marching around the walls. You may be on day five, day six. That simply means you've been doing it a year, two years, or five years. Surely you've thought it would have happened by now.

Pass that test. Don't start complaining. Don't do like the first group that stopped at the door of the Promised Land and said, "Oh, what's the use?

Let's just settle here." When the negative thoughts come, let them die stillborn. Refuse to prophesy defeat over your life. If you do this, you will come in to your seventh day. Like what happened with the Israelites, those walls will come tumbling down. God is a faithful God. He will do what He has promised you.

"IT IS WELL"

In 2 Kings 4, there is a remarkable story of a woman who was a good friend of the prophet Elisha. In fact, she had built an extra room on her house, so when Elisha was in town he could come and stay there. One day Elisha asked her what he could do for her to return the favor. She said, "Nothing, Elisha. My husband and I are doing just fine."

Elisha's assistant brought it to his attention that the couple didn't have any children. Her husband was an older man. Before Elisha left the woman, he prophesied, "By this time next year you're going to have a baby." She was so excited. It seemed too good to be true. But the next year, just like he told her, she had a son. When the boy was around ten years old, he was out in the field playing and his head began to hurt very badly. They carried him home and placed him in his mother's arms where he later died. You can imagine how this mother felt. She was heartbroken, devastated beyond measure. She carried her son to Elisha's room and placed him on Elisha's bed.

For most people this would be the end of the story, but not for this lady. She asked for a donkey and said, "I'm going to see the prophet Elisha." She told her assistant to ride fast and not slow down unless he was told. When Elisha saw the dust billowing up in the sky a couple of miles away, he noticed it was his friend, the woman who had built the extra room on her house for him. Elisha told his assistant Gehazi, "Go find out what's wrong."

Gehazi ran to meet the woman way down the road, stopped her, and said, "Elisha is concerned. Why are you coming unexpectedly in such a hurry? Is it well with you? Is it well with your husband? Is it well with the child?"

Speaking words of faith, she simply replied, "It is well," and kept heading full steam ahead.

Think of all the negative thoughts that this woman was fighting, and then consider her actual words. A lot of times when we face difficulties and somebody asks us how everything is going, we do just the opposite and tell them everything that's wrong. It's easy to talk about the problem, how bad it is, how it's never going to work out. But in those tough times—when you feel like complaining, when you've got a good reason to be sour, because you lost a job, or a friend did you wrong, or you're not feeling well—you have to dig your heels in and say it by faith: "Business is slow, but all is well. God is still on the throne. He's the Lord my Provider." Or, "The medical report wasn't good, but all is well. God is my healer. Nothing will snatch me out of His hands."

She finally made it to Elisha's house and told him the son he promised her had died. Elisha went and prayed for the boy, and he came back to life. What I want you to see is that in her darkest hour, even when it looked impossible, this lady refused to get negative and speak defeat. When Gehazi asked, "Is everything okay?" she could have spoken out what I'm sure she was thinking, "No! I'm in the midst of a great tragedy. I'm facing the biggest challenge of my life." Nobody would have faulted her for that. But she chose to speak faith even though her mind was being bombarded with doubt. She had a watch over her mouth. She wasn't going to be snared by her words.

When you're hurting, you've been through a disappointment, and you've suffered a loss, you have to do what she did. Say it by faith, "All is well." It may not look well. It may not feel well. In the natural you should be complaining, talking about how bad it is, but instead you're making a declaration of faith: "All is well." That's when the most powerful force in the universe goes to work.

EVERY WALL WILL COME TUMBLING DOWN

God can resurrect dead dreams. He can resurrect a dead marriage. He can resurrect health that's going down or a business that's failing. When you get in agreement with God, all things are possible. You may be facing a big obstacle. It doesn't look good.

But here's a key: Don't talk about the size of your problem. Talk about the size of your God. God stopped the sun for Joshua. He parted the Red Sea for the Israelites. He breathed new life into this mother's little boy. He can turn your situation around as well. He can make a way even though you don't see a way.

My challenge today is: Don't let your negative words stop what God wants to do. If you can't say anything positive, zip it up. You may think it, but don't give it life by speaking it out. Your healing, your vindication, and your promotion are right up in front of you. As was true of Jeremiah, God has already ordained you to do something great. Now, put a watch over your mouth. Pay attention to what you're saying.

When you make this adjustment, God is going to release promises that have been delayed. Suddenly the things you've been praying about—breaking that addiction, meeting the right person, getting healthy again, starting that business—are going to fall into place. You're going to see God's favor in a new way. He's going to open up new doors of opportunity just as He did for Joshua and the Israelites. I believe and declare that every wall that's holding you back is about to come tumbling down. You and your children will make it into your Promised Land!

3

WORDS HAVE CREATIVE POWER

Words have creative power. When you speak something out, you give life to what you're saying. It's one thing to believe that you're blessed. That's important. But when you say, "I am blessed," it takes on a whole new meaning. That's when blessings come looking for you. The Scripture says, "Let the redeemed of the Lord *say so*." It doesn't say, "Let the redeemed think so, or believe so, or hope so." That's all good, but you have to take it one step

further and *say so*. If you're going to go to the next
level, you have to *say so*. If you're going to accomplish a dream, overcome an obstacle, or break an
addiction, you have to start declaring it. It has to
come out of your mouth. That's how you give life
to your faith.

When God created the worlds, He didn't just
think them into being. He didn't just believe there
would be light and land and oceans and animals.
He had it in His heart, but nothing happened until
He spoke. He said, "Let there be light," and light
came. His thoughts didn't set it into motion; His
words set it into motion. It's the same principle
today. You can believe all day long and not see anything happen. You can have faith in your heart, big
dreams, be standing on God's promises, and never
see anything change. What's the problem? Nothing
happens until you speak. Instead of just believing
you're going to get out of debt, you have to say so.
Declare every day, "I am coming out of debt. I am
the head and not the tail. God's favor surrounds
me like a shield." When you speak, just like when

God spoke, things begin to happen. Opportunities will find you. Good breaks, promotion, and ideas will track you down.

Instead of just thinking, *I hope I get over this illness. I'm praying I'll get better,* which is good, you have to take it one more step and start declaring it. "I am strong. I am healthy. I will live and not die. With long life God is going to satisfy me." That's what activates your faith. It's not just hoping you have a good year or just hoping that you accomplish your dreams. Hope is good, but nothing happens until you speak. Before you leave the house every day, declare it: "This is going to be my best year. Things have shifted in my favor. I'm going to a new level." When you talk like that, the angels go to work, opening up new doors, lining up the right people, and arranging things in your favor.

"I WILL SAY"

Psalm 91 says, "I will say of the Lord, 'He is my refuge, my fortress, and my shield.'" The next verse says, "He will deliver me, protect me, and cover me." Notice the connection. *I will say* and *He will do*. It doesn't say, "I believe He is my refuge. I believe He will be my strength." The psalmist went around declaring it, speaking it out: "The Lord is my refuge. The Lord is my strength." Notice what happened. God became his refuge and strength. God was saying in effect, "If you're bold enough to speak it, I'm bold enough to do it."

Have you ever declared that your dreams are coming to pass? Have you ever said, "I will pay off my house" "I will start my own business." "I will get my degree." "I will lose this weight." "I will see my family restored"? Whatever God has put in your heart, it needs to get in your conversation. Talk like it's going to happen. Talk like it's already on the way: "When I get married . . . When I graduate from college . . . When I see my family restored . . ." Not *if* it's going to happen, but *when* it's going to happen. That's your faith being released.

One of our staff members had been trying for more than ten years to have a baby, with no success. One day we were in a staff meeting, planning out the next year. She made the statement, "When I have my baby, I'm going to be out for a couple of months. We'll have to find somebody to fill in." I thought she was pregnant and nobody had told me, so I didn't act surprised or say anything. My sister Lisa was in the meeting as well. I asked her afterward, "Why didn't you tell me she was pregnant?"

She said, "Joel, she's not pregnant. She just talks like it's going to happen."

This went on for years. "When I have my baby . . . When I get pregnant . . . When my child shows up . . ." What was she doing? Saying so. She didn't just believe it. She was declaring it. In the natural, she was getting too old to have a baby. Her doctors told her it wasn't going to happen. It looked impossible. Most people would have given up and accepted it. But not this lady. She kept saying so, kept declaring it: "When my baby shows up . . ." Twenty years later, she gave birth not to one baby but to two. She had twins. She declared of the Lord and God did what He promised.

But think about the opposite of Psalm 91, "I will not say of the Lord, and He will not do." That's the principle. Nothing happens until you speak.

WHAT ARE YOU SAYING?

When we were trying to acquire the Compaq Center to become our church building, Victoria and I would drive around it night after night and say, "That's our building. Father, thank You for fighting our battles. Lord, thank You that You are making a way where we don't see a way." We didn't just think about it, pray about it, or believe that it would happen. That's all important, but we took one more step and declared that it was ours. It became a part of our everyday conversation. At the dinner table: "When we get the Compaq Center, we could do this. When we renovate it . . . When we move in . . . When we have the grand opening . . ." Not, "I don't know, Victoria. It's going to be very expensive. Where are we going to get the funds? The opponents, they're really strong." No, we said of the Lord, as the psalmist did, "God, we know You are bigger than any obstacle. We know You are supplying all of our needs. Lord, we know if You be for us, who dare be against us?" We declared it, and God did it.

What are you saying of the Lord? "Well, Joel. My problems are really big today. My dreams look impossible. My marriage is so messed up. We'll never be restored." Don't talk about how big your problem is. Talk about how big your God is. When you say of the Lord, "You're my healer, my way maker, my dream giver, my restorer, my vindicator, my health, my peace, my victory," that's when God will show up and do more than you can ask or think.

I have some friends who were believing to have another child. They have a daughter, but they really wanted to have a son. Every time the wife got pregnant, she had a miscarriage. This happened five times in nine years. They were very discouraged and tempted to give up. The husband's name is Joe and had gone by Joe his whole life. But one day he read that his full name—Joseph—means "God will add." When he understood that, something came alive inside. He knew God was saying, "I'm going to add to you a son." He remembered the story in the Scripture where God changed Abram's name to Abraham, which means "father of many nations." God gave Abraham a child, a son, at a very old age when it looked impossible. Joe decided to go back to using his original name. He told his family, his friends, and coworkers, "Don't call me Joe anymore. Call me Joseph."

They thought he was having a midlife crisis. But every time someone said, "Hello, Joseph," they were saying, "God will add." They were speaking victory over his life. He kept saying so, declaring it. About six months later, his wife became pregnant with a baby boy. For the first time in ten years, she carried the baby to full term. Their son was born healthy and whole. As a testimony to God's goodness, they named that little boy Joseph: "God will add."

WHATEVER GOD HAS PUT IN YOUR HEART

Are you declaring victory over your life, over your family, over your career? Nothing happens until you speak. When you get up in the morning, you need to make some declarations of faith. Whatever God has put in your heart, declare that it will come to pass. I say every day, "I am increasing in the anointing, in wisdom, in favor, and in influence. Every message is getting better. God is taking our ministry where no ministry has ever gone." You have to speak favor into your future. I declare every day, "My children will fulfill their destinies. Their gifts and talents will come out to the full. They will supersede anything that we've done."

Ever since I took over for my father in the church, I have said, "When people turn on the television and see me, they cannot turn me off." Do you know how many letters I get from people who say, "Joel, I was flipping through the channels. I don't like TV preachers. I never watch TV preachers, but when I turned you on, I couldn't turn you off"?

I think to myself, *I called you in! I said so.*

One man wrote and told how his wife tried to get him to watch the program for many years, but he wouldn't do it. One day he was flipping through the channels and came across our program. Normally he would flip by it very quickly. But for some reason this day his remote control stopped working, and he got stuck on our program. He was so frustrated. He finagled with the remote and ended up changing the batteries. It still wouldn't work. He said, "Joel, even though I tried to act like I wasn't listening, you were speaking directly to me." The funny thing is, when our program was over, the remote control went back to working just fine. He said, "Now I never miss one of your programs."

When you declare favor over your life and over your future, God will make things happen that should have never happened. Our attitude should be, *I'm coming out of debt, and I'm saying so. This will be my best year, and I'm saying so. I will overcome every obstacle, and I'm saying so. I will accomplish my dreams, and I'm saying so.*

USE YOUR WORDS TO CHANGE THE SITUATION

In the Scripture there was a lady who had been sick for many years. She had gone to the best doctors, spent all of her money trying to get well, but nothing worked. One day she heard Jesus was coming through town. The Scripture says, *"She kept saying to herself."* She wasn't saying, "I'm never going to get well. I can't believe this has happened to me. I always get bad breaks." No, she kept saying to herself, "When I get to Jesus, I know I will be made whole." In the midst of the difficulty, she was prophesying victory. All through the day, over and over, she kept saying, "Healing is on its way. Brighter days are up ahead." When she started making her way to Jesus, it was extremely crowded, but she didn't complain, she didn't get discouraged, and she kept saying, "This is my time. Things are changing in my favor." The more she said it, the closer she got. Finally she reached out and touched the edge of His robe, and she was instantly healed.

Notice the principle: Whatever you're constantly saying, you're moving toward. You may be struggling in your finances, but when you keep declaring, "I am blessed. I am prosperous. I have the favor of God," every time you say it, you're moving toward increase. You're getting closer to seeing that come to pass. You may be facing a sickness. It doesn't look good. But every time you declare, "I am healthy. I am strong. I am getting better," you're moving toward health, wholeness, victory. Perhaps you're struggling with an addiction. Every time you declare, "I am free. This addiction does not control me," you're moving toward freedom. You're moving toward breakthroughs.

Now here's the catch. This works both in the positive and in the negative. If you're always saying, "I am so unlucky. I never get any good breaks," you're moving toward bad breaks, more disappointment. "Joel, my back has been hurting for three years. I don't think I'll ever get well." You're moving toward more sickness, more pain. "Look, I've been through so much. I don't think I'll ever be happy again." You're moving toward more discouragement, more sadness. If you will change what you're saying, you will change what you're seeing. The Scripture says, "Call the things that are not as if they already were."

A lot of times we do just the opposite. We call the things that are as if they will always be that way.

In other words, we just describe the situation. "Gas is so high. I don't see how I'm going to make it." You're calling in more struggle, more lack. "I can't stand my job. My boss gets on my nerves." You're calling in more frustration, more defeat. Don't use your words to describe the situation. Use your words to change the situation.

HAVE A BETTER SAY SO

One time our daughter, Alexandra, had a copy of my first book from ten years ago and a copy of my newest book. She was comparing the photos on the cover. She exclaimed, "Wow, Daddy! You look better today than you did ten years ago." I said, "What would you like me to buy you?"

Do you know how many times I have said, "I'm getting stronger, healthier, wiser. My youth is being renewed like the eagles." Every time you say it, you're moving toward it. But if you're always saying, "I'm so out of shape. I'll never lose this weight," you're moving toward the wrong thing.

A gentleman who looked to be about seventy recently told me, "Joel, when you get old, it's all downhill." That was his *say so*. He was declaring, "I'm going down." He was calling in poor health, lack of vision, and hearing loss. If he keeps that up, he'll keep moving toward it. By the way he looked, he had already been saying it for a long time!

I realize we're all going to get old. We're all eventually going to die, but don't make plans to go downhill. Don't start speaking defeat over your life. Moses was one hundred and twenty years old when he died, and the Scripture says, "His eye was not dim, his natural strength not abated." One hundred and twenty. Healthy. Strong. Twenty-twenty vision. Didn't have reading glasses. Wasn't wearing a "Help! I've fallen and I can't get up" button around his chest! He had a clear memory, a strong, sharp mind. In spite of how you feel, in spite of what's been passed down in your family line, every day you need to declare, "Everything about me is getting better and better—my bones, my joints, my ligaments, my blood, my organs, my memory, my vision, my hearing, my talent, my skill, my looks, my skin. My youth is being renewed. Like Moses, I will finish my course with my eye not dim, my natural strength not abated." You talk like that, and you're moving toward renewed youth, health, energy, and vitality.

That's a lot better than getting up in the morning, looking in the mirror, and saying, "Oh, man, I'm getting so old. Look at these wrinkles. I look so bad. This gray hair. I'm so out of shape." You keep moving toward that, and in five years it's going to be scary! You need to have a better *say so*. Don't talk about the way you are. Talk about the way you want to be. You are prophesying your future.

There's a young lady on staff at Lakewood. Every morning before she leaves her house, she looks in the mirror and says, "Girl, you're looking good today." I saw her one time and asked if she was still doing it. She said, "Yeah, in fact, today when I looked in the mirror, I said, 'Girl, some days you look good; but today, you look *really* good.'"

Why don't you stop criticizing yourself? Stop talking about all the things you don't like—how you're getting too old, too wrinkled, too this, too that. Start calling yourself strong, healthy, talented, beautiful, and young. Every morning, before you leave your house, look in the mirror and say, "Good morning, you good-looking thing!"

TURN IT AROUND

Maybe you're in a difficult time today. To complain, "I don't think I'll ever get out," is just going to draw in more defeat. Your declaration should be, "I have grace for this season. I am strong in the Lord. Those who are for me are greater than those who are against me." When you say that, strength comes. Courage comes. Confidence comes. Endurance comes. If you go through a disappointment, a bad break, or a loss, don't grumble, "I don't know why this has happened to me. It's so unfair." That's just going to draw in more self-pity. Your declaration should be, "God promised me beauty for ashes, joy for mourning. I'm not staying here. I'm moving forward. New beginnings are in my future. The rest of my life will be the best of my life." You talk like that, and you're moving toward double for your trouble. You're moving away from self-pity and toward God's goodness in a new way.

One of the best things we can do is take a few minutes every morning and make these positive declarations over our lives. Write down not only your dreams, your goals, and your vision, but make a list of any area you want to improve in, anything you want to see changed. Put that list on your bathroom mirror, somewhere private. Before you leave the house, take a couple of minutes and declare that over your life. If you struggle with your self-esteem, feeling less than, you need to declare every day, "I am confident. I am valuable. I am one of a kind. I have royal blood flowing through my veins. I am wearing a crown of favor. I am a child of the Most High God." You declare that, and you'll go out with your shoulders back, with your head held high.

If you struggle with your weight, declare, "I am in shape. I am healthy. I'm full of energy. I weigh what I should weigh." It may not be true right now, but you keep saying it and you're going to move toward it.

Instead of living under a blanket of guilt and condemnation and being focused on past mistakes, declare, "I am forgiven. I am redeemed. I am wearing a robe of righteousness. God is pleased with me."

The Scripture says, "Let the weak say, 'I am strong.'" It doesn't say, "Let the weak talk about the weakness. Discuss the weakness. Call five friends and explain the weakness." You have to send your words out in the direction you want your life to go.

When you're in a tough time and somebody asks you how you're doing, don't go through a sad song of everything that's wrong in your life. "Oh, man, my back's been hurting. Traffic is so bad today. My boss isn't treating me right. The dishwasher broke. The goldfish died, and my dog doesn't like me." All that's going to do is draw in more defeat. Turn it around. Have a report of victory. "I am blessed. I am healthy. I am prosperous. I have the favor of God." What you consistently talk about, you're moving toward.

TALK TO THE MOUNTAIN

This is what David did. When he faced Goliath, it looked impossible. All the odds were against him. He could have easily gone around saying, "I know

I'm supposed to face Goliath, but look at him. He's twice my size. He's got more experience, more equipment, more talent. I don't see how this is ever going to work out." You can talk yourself out of your destiny. Negative words can keep you from becoming who you were created to be. David looked Goliath in the eyes and said, "You come against me with a sword and a shield. But I come against you in the name of the Lord God of Israel. This day, I will defeat you and feed your head to the birds of the air!" Notice he was prophesying victory. He may have felt fear, but he spoke faith. I can hear David, as he's going out to face Goliath, affirming under his breath, "I am well able. I am anointed. I am equipped. If God be for me, who dare be against me?" He picked up that rock, slung it in his slingshot, and Goliath came tumbling down.

When you face giants in life, you have to do as David did and prophesy your future. "Cancer, you are no match for me. I will defeat you." "This addiction may have been in my family for years, but this is a new day. The buck stops with me. I'm the difference maker. I am free." "My child may have been off course for a long time, but I know it's only temporary. As for me and my house, we will serve the Lord."

There was a man in the Scripture named Zerubbabel. He faced a huge mountain. To rebuild the temple in Jerusalem was a big obstacle, with enemies opposing every step. But like David, he didn't talk about how impossible it was, how it was never going to work out. He said, "Who are you, oh great mountain, that would stand before me? You shall become a mere molehill." He was prophesying his future. The mountain looked big. But he declared it would be flattened out. It would become a molehill. Here's the principle: Don't talk about the mountain; talk to the mountain. Look at that mountain of debt and tell it, "You can't defeat me. You're coming down. I will lend and not borrow. My cup will run over." Whatever mountains you face in life, no matter how big they look, don't shrink back in fear or be intimidated. Rise up in faith and tell that mountain, "You're coming down." Tell that sickness, "You're temporary."

Say to that loneliness, that addiction, that legal problem, "Who are you, oh great mountain, to stand before me?" In other words, "Don't you know who I am? A child of the Most High God. Haven't you read my birth certificate? My Father created the universe. He breathed life into me and crowned me with His favor. He called me more than a conqueror. That means you can't defeat me. You can't hold me back. Oh great mountain, you've got to come down. I will overcome this illness. I will break this addiction. I will pay my house off. I will see my family restored. I will accomplish my dreams."

Prophesy victory. Prophesy breakthroughs. Prophesy what you're believing for.

RESURRECT
WHAT LOOKS DEAD

In the Old Testament, Ezekiel saw a vision. He had this dream of a valley filled with bones. It was like a huge graveyard. Everywhere he looked was acres and acres of bones from people who had died. Bones represent things in our life that look dead, situations that seem impossible and permanently unchanging. God told him to do something interesting. He said, "Ezekiel, prophesy to these dead bones. Say to them, 'Oh, you dry bones, hear the word of the Lord.'" Ezekiel, in this vision, started speaking to the bones, telling them to come back to life. He called in skin, muscle, and tissue. As he was speaking, the bones started rattling and coming together, just like out of a movie, morphing back into a person. Finally, God told him to "prophesy to the breath" and call it forth. The Scripture says, "As he prophesied, breath came into those bodies, and they stood up like a vast army."

You may have things in your life that seem dead—a relationship, a business, your health. All you can see is a valley of dry bones, so to speak. God is saying to you what He said to Ezekiel. It's not enough to just pray about it; you need to speak to it. Prophesy to those dead bones. Call in health. Call in abundance. Call in restoration. That child who's been off course, don't just pray about him or her. Prophesy and say, "Son, daughter, come back in. You will fulfill your destiny." If you're struggling with an addiction, don't just pray about it, but prophesy. "I am free. Chains are broken off me. This is a new day of victory." Get your checkbook out and prophesy to it. All it looks like are dead bones. Debt. Lack. Struggle. "I prophesy to these dead bones that I will lend and not borrow. I am the head and not the tail. I am coming in to overflow." Just as with Ezekiel, if you'll prophesy to the bones, God will resurrect what looks dead. He'll make things happen that you could never make happen.

A friend of mine smoked cigarettes from an early age. She had tried again and again to stop but couldn't do it. She was constantly saying, "I'll never break this addiction. It's too hard. And if I do, I know I'll gain so much weight." This went on for years. One day someone told her what I'm telling you, to change what she was saying, to prophesy victory. She started saying, "I don't like to smoke.

I can't stand the taste of nicotine. I'm going to quit and not gain any extra weight." She said that day after day. Even when she was smoking and enjoying it, she would say, "I can't stand to smoke." She wasn't talking about the way she was. She was talking about the way she wanted to be. About three months later, one morning she noticed the cigarette tasted funny, almost bitter. She thought she got a bad pack. It got worse and worse. Several months later, it had gotten so bad she couldn't stand it anymore. She stopped smoking, and she never gained one extra pound. Today she is totally free. She broke that addiction, in part, by the power of her words. She prophesied her future.

Maybe like her, you've spent years saying negative things over your life. "I can't break this addiction. My marriage is never going to make it. I'll never get out of debt." You have to send your words out in a new direction. You are prophesying the wrong thing. Get in a habit of making these positive declarations over your life. Every day declare that your dreams are coming to pass. It's not enough to just believe it. Nothing happens until you speak. As was true of the psalmist, when you say of the Lord, God will do what He promised.

PERSONAL "SAY SO"S

Let me lead you in a few "Say So"s. Make these declarations out loud.

"I will accomplish my dreams. The right people are in my future. The right opportunities are headed my way. Blessings are chasing me down."

"I am the head and not the tail. I will lend and not borrow."

"I have a good personality. I am well liked. I am fun to be around. I enjoy my life. I have a positive outlook."

"I will overcome every obstacle. I will outlast every adversity. Things have shifted in my favor. What was meant for my harm, God is using for my advantage. My future is bright."

"My children are mighty in the land. My legacy will live on to inspire future generations."

"I run with purpose in every step. My best days are still out in front of me. My greatest victories are in my future. I will become everything I was created to be. I will have everything God intended for me to have. I am the redeemed of the Lord, and I *say so* today!"

START DECLARING
LIFE-CHANGING
WORDS

In 1981, my mother was diagnosed with cancer and given just a few weeks to live. I'll never forget what a shock that news was to our family. I had never seen my mother sick one day in all my life. She was extremely healthy and active. She loved being outdoors, working in the yard, working in her flowerbeds.

I was away at college when the doctor's report came. My brother, Paul, called me and said, "Joel, Mother is very, very sick."

"What do you mean, Paul? Does she have the flu or something like that?"

"No, Joel," Paul replied. "She's losing weight. Her skin is yellow, and she's extremely weak; something is seriously wrong with her."

Mother was hospitalized for twenty-one days, while the doctors ran test after test. They sent her lab work all over the country, hoping to find some key to help her. Finally, they came back with the dreaded report that she had metastatic cancer of the liver. They called my dad out into the hallway and said, "Pastor, we hate to tell you this, but your wife has only a few weeks to live. Not months, weeks . . ."

Medical science had reached the limits of what they could do. The best and brightest doctors in the world had exhausted their efforts, so they basically sent our mom home to die.

We expressed our sincere appreciation to the doctors and hospital staff for their hard work, but we refused to accept their opinions. I'm grateful for doctors, hospitals, medicine, and science, but the medical professionals can present only what their medical charts tell them. Thank God, you and I can appeal to a higher Authority. We can always have another report. God's report says, "I will restore health to you and heal your wounds."

We serve a supernatural God. He is not limited to the laws of nature. He can do what human beings cannot do. He can make a way in our lives where it looks as if there is no way. That's what we prayed that He would do in Mother's life.

And my mother never gave up. She refused to speak words of defeat. She didn't complain about how sick or weak she felt, or how awful her life was, or how hopeless her situation looked. She chose to put God's words in her mind and in her mouth.

She started speaking faith-filled words. She started calling in health and calling in healing. All during the day, we'd hear her going through the house speaking aloud, "I will live and not die, and I will declare the works of the Lord." She was like a walking Bible!

I'd say, "Mother, how are you doing?"

She'd say, "Joel, I am strong in the Lord and the power of His might." She pored over her Bible and found about thirty or forty favorite passages of Scripture concerning healing. She wrote them down, and every day, she'd read over them and boldly declare them aloud. We'd see her walking up and down the driveway, saying, "With long life, He satisfies me and shows me His salvation."

Mother mixed her words with God's Words, and something powerful began to happen. Her circumstances began to change. Not overnight, but little by little, she began to feel better. She got her appetite back and started gaining weight. Slowly but surely, her strength returned.

What was happening? God was watching over His Word to perform it. God was restoring health to her and healing her of her wounds. A few weeks went by and Mother got a little better. A few months went by, and she was even better. A few years went by, and she just kept on confessing God's Word. Today, it has been more than thirty-seven years since we received the report that Mother had just a few weeks to live, and as I write these words, Mother is totally free from that cancer, healed by the power of God's Word!

And she is still confessing God's Word. She gets up every morning and reviews those same Scriptures on the subject of healing. She still speaks those words of faith, victory, and health over her life. She won't leave the house until she does it. Beyond that, she loves to remind "Mr. Death" that he has no hold on her life. Every time my mother passes a graveyard, she literally shouts out loud, "With long life He satisfies me and shows me His salvation!" The first time she did that when I was riding in the car with her, I nearly jumped out of my seat!

But Mother refuses to give the enemy a foothold.

BOLDLY CONFESS
GOD'S WORD

Mother used her words to change her world, and you can do the same thing. Maybe you are facing a "hopeless" situation. Don't give up. God is a miracle-working God. He knows what you're going through, and He will not let you down. He is a friend that sticks closer than a brother. If you will trust in Him and start speaking words of faith, your circumstances will begin to change.

Of course, we don't have to be in life-threatening situations to use God's Word. We can speak God's Word in our everyday lives. Parents, you ought to speak God's Word over your children every day before they go to school. Just say, "Father, You promised me in Psalm 91 that You will give Your angels charge over us and that no evil would come near our household. So I thank You that my children are supernaturally protected, and You are guiding them and watching after them. Father, You said that we're the head and not the tail, and You will surround us with favor. So I thank You that my children are blessed, and they will excel at whatever they put their hands to do."

Speaking God's Word over your children can make an enormous difference in their lives. I know my mother prayed over my siblings and me every day before we went to school. She prayed specifically that we'd never break any bones. She raised five healthy, very active children. We all played sports and did a lot of crazy things, but to this day, as far as I know, not one of us has ever broken a bone.

Just as it is imperative that we see ourselves as God sees us and think about ourselves as God regards us, it is equally important that we say about ourselves what God says about us. Our words are vital in bringing our dreams to pass. It's not enough to simply see it by faith or in your imagination. You have to begin speaking words of faith over your life. Your words have enormous creative power. The moment you speak something out, you give birth to it. This is a spiritual principle, and it works whether what you are saying is good or bad, positive or negative.

In that regard, many times we are our own worst enemies. We blame everybody and everything else, but the truth is, we are profoundly influenced by what we say about ourselves. Remember the Scripture says, "We are snared by the words of our mouth."

"Nothing good ever happens to me. My dreams never come to pass. I knew I wouldn't get promoted." Statements such as these will literally prevent you from moving ahead in life. That's why you must learn to guard your tongue and speak only faith-filled words over your life. This is one of the most important principles you can ever grab hold of. Simply put, your words can either make you or break you.

God never commanded us to repeatedly verbalize our pain and suffering. He didn't instruct us to go around discussing our negative situations, airing our "dirty laundry" with all our friends and neighbors. Instead, God told us to speak constantly of His goodness, to speak of His promises in the morning at the breakfast table, in the evenings around the dinner table, at night before bedtime, continually dwelling on the good things of God.

You could experience a new sense of joy in your home, if you'd simply stop talking about the negative things in your life and begin talking about God's Word.

If you are always talking about your problems, don't be surprised if you live in perpetual defeat. If you're in the habit of saying, "Nothing good ever happens to me," guess what? Nothing good is going to happen to you! You must stop talking about the problem and start talking about the solution. Quit speaking words of defeat, and start speaking words of victory. Don't use your words to describe your situation; use your words to change your situation.

Every morning, when I get out of bed, I say, "Father, I thank You that I am strong in the Lord and the power of Your might. I am well able to do what You have called me to do." I quote several other passages of Scripture regarding God's favor in my life. What am I doing? I am starting off my day on a positive note, aligning my thoughts and words with His.

Set the tone for the entire day as soon as you get out of bed. If you wait until you have checked social media or read the morning news, you'll start your day with all sorts of sad, dreary news. Try starting your day with some good news by speaking God's

Word over your life! Don't wait till you've checked the stock report, or you'll be up one day and down the next. The moment you wake up, begin to give new life to your dreams by speaking words of faith and victory.

Understand, avoiding negative talk is not enough. That's similar to a football team having a good defense but no offense. If your team is constantly playing defense, you stand little chance of scoring. You must get the ball and move it down the field; you must get on the offense. You have to be aggressive.

Similarly, you must start boldly confessing God's Word, using your words to move forward in life, to bring to life the great things God has in store for you. The Scripture says, "With the heart one believes unto righteousness, and with the mouth confession is made unto salvation." This same principle is true in other areas. When you believe God's Word and begin to speak it, mixing it with your faith, you are actually confirming that truth and making it valid in your own life.

If you are facing sickness today, you should confirm God's Word concerning healing. Say something such as, "Father, I thank You that You promised me in Psalms that I will live and not die and I will declare the works of the Lord." As you boldly declare it, you are confirming that truth in your own life.

If you are struggling financially, instead of talking about the problem, you need to boldly declare, "Everything I put my hands to prospers and succeeds!"

When you make those kinds of bold declarations, all heaven comes to attention to back up God's Word.

God has not given us hundreds of promises simply for us to read and enjoy. God has given us His promises so we might boldly declare them to bring us victory, health, hope, and abundant life.

In 1997, Victoria and I had the opportunity to develop the last full power television station available in Houston, channel 55. It was a tremendous opportunity but also an enormous undertaking. All we had was a construction permit, basically, a piece of paper giving us the right to build the station. We didn't have a studio, we didn't have a transmitter or a tower to put it on; oh, and we had no programming! We were starting totally from scratch. And we had less than a year to get the station on the air or we'd lose the license. We really needed God's supernatural wisdom to deal with the day-to-day details of building a television station.

I decided to do what my mother did, and every morning when I read my Bible, I wrote down any verse or passage of Scripture that had to do with wisdom or guidance. After a couple of weeks, I had recorded twenty or thirty passages, and every day, before we would leave the house, Victoria and I would read those Scriptures and boldly declare them.

One of my favorite passages was: "For the Lord grants wisdom! His every word is a treasure of knowledge and understanding. He grants good sense to the godly—His saints. He is their shield, protecting them and guarding their pathway. He shows how to distinguish right from wrong, how to make the right decision every time." We'd say, "Father, we thank You that we have Your supernatural wisdom, and we do have the ability to make the right decision every time. Father, You said the steps of a good man are ordered by the Lord, so we thank You that You are guiding and directing our steps." And I cannot tell you how many times during the development of that television station God supernaturally protected us and kept us from making mistakes.

For instance, I was just about to pick up the phone and order an extremely expensive and critical piece of equipment, probably the most important piece of equipment in a television station. Just before I did, a man called me out of the clear blue, and we discussed numerous issues. Toward the end of our conversation, he said something that gave me insight and totally changed the decision I was about to make.

What was happening? God was using that man to help guide us; God was protecting us from making a poor decision, and He was giving us good sense to make the correct decision. God was watching over His Word to perform it.

God wants to do something similar for you, but you can't be lazy. Search the Scriptures and highlight those that particularly apply to your life situation. Write them down and get in the habit of declaring them.

God has already done everything He's going to do. The ball is now in your court. If you want success, if you want wisdom, if you want to be prosperous and healthy, you're going to have to do more than meditate and believe; you must boldly declare words of faith and victory over yourself and your family.

SPEAK WORDS
OF BLESSING

As parents, we can profoundly influence the direction of our children's lives by the words we say to them. I believe as husbands and wives we can set the direction for our entire family. As a business owner, you can help set the direction for your employees. With our words, we have the ability to help mold and shape the future of anyone over whom we have influence.

And each of us has influence over somebody. You may not consider yourself a leader, but you have a sphere of influence nonetheless—somebody or some group that looks up to you. Even if you're a teenager, somebody values your opinion. It is vital that we speak "good things" into the lives of those over whom we have influence. That doesn't mean we will never disagree with them or have to confront and correct them. But the general tenor of our words to them and about them should be positive.

A well-meaning mother was constantly nagging her teenage son. "You're so lazy; you're never going to amount to anything! If you don't shape up, you're never going to get into college. You'll probably wind up getting into trouble."

Those kinds of negative words will destroy a person quicker than you can imagine. You cannot speak negatively about someone on one hand, then turn around and expect that person to be blessed. If you want your son or daughter to be productive and successful, you need to begin declaring words of life over your children rather than predictions of doom and despair. The Scripture reminds us that with our words we can bless people or we can curse them.

In the Old Testament, the people clearly understood the power of the blessing. As the family patri-
arch approached senility or death, the oldest sons
gathered alongside their father. The father would
then lay his hands on each son's head and speak
loving, faith-filled words over them about their
future. These pronouncements comprised what was
known ever after as "the blessing." The family realized that these were more than Dad's dying wishes;
these words carried spiritual authority and had the
ability to bring success, prosperity, and health into
their future.

Many times, children even fought over the
father's blessing. They weren't fighting over money
that they might inherit. Nor were they arguing over
the family business. No, they were fighting over
faith-filled words. They realized that if they received
the father's blessing, wealth and success would be
a natural by-product. Beyond that, they deeply
desired the blessing from somebody they loved and
respected.

One of the most amazing biblical records concerning the power of the blessing comes out of the

lives of Jacob and Esau, the two sons of Isaac. Jacob wanted his father's blessing—not just any blessing, but the blessing that rightfully belonged to the first-born son in the family. Isaac was old, near death, and he was practically blind. One day he called in his son Esau and said, "Esau, go kill some game, and prepare me a meal and I will give you the bless-ing that belongs to the firstborn son." But Jacob's mother, Rachel, overheard this conversation. Rachel loved Jacob more than she loved Esau, so she told Jacob to put on Esau's clothes in an attempt to trick Isaac into giving him the blessing. Then she pre-pared one of Isaac's favorite meals.

While Esau was out in the field hunting, she said to Jacob, "Go to your father and present him this food. And he'll give you the blessing that really belongs to your brother."

Jacob recognized the seriousness of this duplic-ity. He said, "But Mother, what if he finds out that I'm lying, and he curses me instead of blesses me? I'll be cursed for the rest of my life!"

Think about that. Jacob understood that he was risking his entire future on this gambit. He recognized that the words his father spoke over him would impact him, for either good or evil, the rest of his life.

DECLARE GOD'S FAVOR

Whether we realize it or not, our words affect our children's future for either good or evil. Our words have the same kind of power that Isaac's words had. We need to speak loving words of approval and acceptance, words that encourage, inspire, and motivate our children to reach for new heights. When we do that, we are speaking blessings into their lives. We are speaking abundance and increase. We're declaring God's favor in their lives.

But too often, we slip into being harsh and critical with our children, constantly finding fault in something our children are doing. "Why can't you make better grades? You didn't mow the lawn right. Go clean your room—it looks like a pigpen! You can't do anything right, can you?"

Such negative words will cause our children to lose the sense of value God has placed within them. As parents, we do have a responsibility before God and society to train our children, to discipline them when they disobey, to lovingly correct them when they make wrong choices. But we should not constantly harp on our kids. If you continually speak words that discourage and dishearten, before long you will destroy your child's self-image. And with your negative words, you will open a door, allowing the enemy to bring all kinds of insecurity and inferiority into your child's life. Millions of adults today are still suffering as a result of the negative words their parents spoke over them as children.

Remember, if you make the mistake of constantly speaking negative words over your children, you are cursing their future. Moreover, God will hold you responsible for destroying their destiny. With authority comes responsibility, and you have the responsibility as the spiritual authority over your child to make sure that he feels loved, accepted, and approved. You have the responsibility to bless your children.

Beyond that, most children get their concepts of who God is and what He is like from their fathers. If their father is mean, critical, and harsh, inevitably the children will grow up with a distorted view of God. If the father is loving, kind, compassionate, and just, the child will better understand God's character.

One of the reasons I talk so much about the goodness of God is because I saw it modeled by my dad. Nobody could have represented God any better to us Osteen kids than my dad did. Even when we made mistakes or got off track, while Daddy was firm, he was also loving and kind. He nurtured us back to the right course. He never beat us into line; he loved us into line. Although he was very busy, he always took time for us. He encouraged us to do great things, to fulfill our dreams. He used to say, "Joel, don't do what I want you to do. Do what you want to do. Follow your own dreams."

Daddy believed in my brother and sisters and me. He told us we were great, even when we knew we weren't. He referred to us as blessings when we knew we weren't acting as blessings. Sometimes we'd make him mad, and he'd say, "I'm about to beat a little blessing to death!"

Mother and Daddy raised five children in our home. When we were growing up, we didn't have children's church programs such as many churches now have. We all met in the same auditorium. My little sister, April, and I used to sit on the front row of that little feedstore that held about two hundred people. We'd play tic-tac-toe the whole service. (I'm confessing to let you know there's still hope for your children. I didn't pay attention, and God made me a pastor. Who knows what God is going to do with your children!)

Daddy would be up on the platform, and Mother would have all five of us kids lined up in a row. She'd have her hands raised in the air, worshiping God with her eyes completely closed. Yet she had an incredible ability, even with her eyes closed, to know when we kids were cutting up. That amazed me. I think that was my first experience with the supernatural power of God! I'd watch Mother to make sure that her eyes were closed before I'd do something to aggravate my brother, Paul. Without missing a beat, Mother would slowly bring one hand down, very gracefully grab my arm, and pinch the fire out of me! I wanted to scream, but I knew better. And then she'd lift that arm back up and continue worshiping the Lord.

I used to think, *Mama, you have a gift. That's supernatural!*

I'm joking (a little), but the point is my siblings and I were not perfect kids. We made plenty of mistakes. But my parents never focused on our weaknesses or on the problems. They always focused on the solutions. They constantly told us we were the best kids in the world. And we grew up secure, knowing that our parents not only loved each other, but they loved us and believed in us. They were going to stand behind us through thick and thin. We knew they were never going to criticize or condemn us, but would always believe the best in us.

Because I grew up with acceptance and approval from my parents, now, as a father myself, I'm practicing the same sort of things with my children. I'm speaking words of blessing into their lives that will be passed down to another generation. And I know my children will pass down the goodness of God to their children, and on and on.

One of the first things I did when I saw my son, Jonathan, in the morning is to say, "Jonathan, you're the best." I'm constantly telling him, "Jonathan, you are God's gift to Mother and me. We love you. We're proud of you. We'll always stand behind you." I tell our daughter, Alexandra, the same sort of things.

Before they went to bed, I told both of our children, "Daddy will always be your best friend." Victoria and I constantly tell them, "There's nothing you can't do. You have a bright future in front of you. You're surrounded by God's favor. Everything you touch is going to prosper." Victoria and I believe that we had an opportunity and a responsibility to speak God's blessings into our children now, while they were young. Why should we have waited till they were teenagers, or in their twenties and about to get married, to begin praying for God's blessings in their lives? No, we're declaring God's blessings over them all the days of their lives. And we are convinced that our words will impact our children long after they are grown and have children of their own.

What are you passing down to the next generation? It's not enough to think it; you must vocalize it. A blessing is not a blessing until it is spoken. Your children need to hear you say words such as, "I love you. I believe in you. I think you're great. There's nobody else like you. You are one of a kind." They need to hear your approval. They need to feel your love. They need your blessing.

Your children may be grown and gone, but that shouldn't stop you from picking up the phone to call and encourage them, to tell them you are proud of them. Maybe you didn't do well at blessing your children as they were growing up. It's not too late. Start to do it now.

WORDS CAN'T BE TAKEN BACK

Jacob stood before his nearly blind father, Isaac, pretending to be his brother, Esau. Although Isaac's eyesight was dim, his intellect was not. He questioned, "Esau, is that really you?"

"Yes, Father; it's me," Jacob lied.

Isaac wasn't convinced, so he called his son closer to him. Only when he smelled Esau's clothes that Jacob was wearing was he finally convinced. He then gave Jacob the blessing that really belonged to his older brother. He said something like this: "May you always have an abundance of grain and an abundance of wine. May nations bow low before you and people always serve you. May you be the lord over your brothers. May anyone that curses you be cursed, and anyone that blesses you be blessed." Notice, in Isaac's blessing he declared great things concerning Jacob's future, and a study of history will show that those things came to pass.

On the other hand, shortly after Jacob left the room, Esau came in. He said, "Dad, sit up; I've got the meal I've prepared for you."

Now Isaac was confused. He said, "Who are you?"

"Dad, I'm Esau, your firstborn son." At that point, the Bible records that Isaac began to shake violently. He realized that he had been duped. He explained to Esau how his brother, Jacob, had come in and deceitfully tricked him out of his blessing.

Now, here's an amazing aspect of this awful story of treachery. Esau began to cry with a loud voice, saying, "Father, can't you still give me the blessing that belongs to the firstborn?"

Isaac's answer was insightful and powerful: "No, the words have already gone forth, and I cannot take them back. I said that Jacob will be blessed, and he will always be blessed."

Do you see the power of our words? Do you see the power of speaking blessings over your children? Isaac said, "Once the words go forth, I can't take them back." He gave Esau a lesser blessing, but it was not nearly as significant as the one he had given to Jacob.

We need to be extremely careful about what we allow to come out of our mouths. The next time you're tempted to talk down to somebody, to belittle your child or degrade him, remember, you can't ever get those words back. Once you speak them, they take on a life of their own.

Use your words to speak blessings over people. Quit criticizing your child and start declaring great things in store for her future.

We should never speak negative destructive words toward anybody, especially toward people over whom we have authority or influence. Just because you have your own business or supervise a large number of employees doesn't give you the right to talk down to them and make them feel badly about themselves. Quite the contrary! God is going to hold you accountable for what you say to those individuals under your authority, and He is going to judge you by a stricter standard. You should go out of your way to speak positive words that build up and encourage.

Similarly, it is important for a husband to understand that his words have tremendous power in his wife's life. He needs to bless her with his words. She's given her life to love and care for him, to partner with him, to create a family together, to nurture his children. If he is always finding fault in something she's doing, always putting her down, he will reap horrendous problems in his marriage and in his life. Moreover, many women today are depressed and feel emotionally abused because their husbands do not bless them with their words. One of the leading causes of emotional breakdowns among married women is the fact that women do not feel valued. One of the main reasons for that deficiency is because husbands are willfully or unwittingly withholding the words of approval women so desperately desire. If you want to see God do wonders in your marriage, start praising your spouse. Start appreciating and encouraging her.

"Oh, my wife knows I love her," one elderly fellow said. "I don't need to tell her. I told her back when we got married forty-two years ago."

No, she needs to hear it again and again. Every single day, a husband should tell his wife, "I love you. I appreciate you. You're the best thing that ever happened to me." A wife should do the same for her husband. Your relationship would improve immensely if you'd simply start speaking kind, positive words, blessing your spouse instead of cursing him or her.

DECLARE GOD'S GOODNESS

You must start declaring God's goodness in your life. Start boldly declaring, "God's face is smiling toward me, and He longs to be good to me." That is not bragging. That is how God says we're going to be blessed—when we start declaring His goodness.

Allow me to make some declarations in your life:

- *I declare that you are blessed with God's supernatural wisdom, and you have clear direction for your life.*
- *I declare that you are blessed with creativity, with courage, with ability, and with abundance.*
- *I declare that you are blessed with a strong will and with self-control and self-discipline.*
- *I declare that you are blessed with a great family, with good friends, with good health, and with faith, favor, and fulfillment.*
- *I declare that you are blessed with success, with supernatural strength, with promotion, and with divine protection.*
- *I declare that you are blessed with an obedient heart and with a positive outlook on life.*

- *I declare that any curse that has ever been spoken over you, any negative evil word that has ever come against you, is broken right now.*
- *I declare that you are blessed in the city. You are blessed in the country. You are blessed when you go in. You are blessed when you come out.*
- *I declare that everything you put your hands to do is going to prosper and succeed.*
- *I declare that you are blessed!*

I encourage you to receive these words and meditate on them; let them sink down deeply into your heart and mind and become a reality in your life. Practice doing something similar with your family. Learn to speak blessings over your life, your friends, your future. Remember, a blessing is not a blessing until it is spoken. If you'll do your part and start boldly speaking blessings over your life and the lives of those around you, God will provide everything you need to live the life of abundance He wants you to have.

ABOUT THE AUTHOR

JOEL OSTEEN is the senior pastor of Lakewood Church in Houston, Texas. More than 10 million viewers watch his weekly-televised services each week in the United States, and millions more in 100 nations around the world. He can also be heard 24 hours a day on Joel Osteen Radio SiriusXM channel 128. He is the author of 11 national bestselling books and has been named by numerous publications as one of the most influential Christian leaders in the world. He resides in Houston with his wife, Victoria, and their children. You can visit his website at http://www.joelosteen.com.

Stay connected, be blessed.

Get more from Joel & Victoria Osteen

It's time to step into the life of victory and favor that God has planned for you! Featuring new messages from Joel & Victoria Osteen, their free daily devotional and inspiring articles, hope is always at your fingertips with the free Joel Osteen app and online at JoelOsteen.com.

Get the app and visit us today at JoelOsteen.com.

CONNECT WITH US